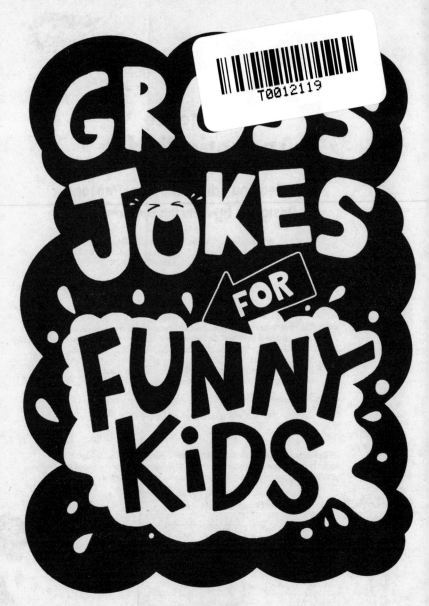

GROSS JOKES FOR FUNNY KIDS

BUSTER BOOKS

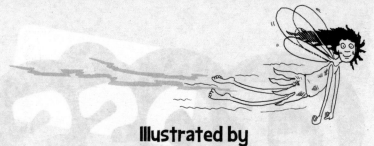

Illustrated by
Andrew Pinder

Compiled and edited by Gary Panton
Designed by Derrian Bradder

First published in Great Britain in 2023 by Buster Books,
an imprint of Michael O'Mara Books Limited,
9 Lion Yard, Tremadoc Road, London SW4 7NQ

W www.mombooks.com/buster f Buster Books 🐦 @BusterBooks 📷 @buster_books

A CIP catalogue record for this book is available from the British Library.

ISBN: 978-1-78055-943-8

2 4 6 8 10 9 7 5 3 1

This product is made of material from well-managed, FSC®-certified
forests and other controlled sources. The manufacturing processes
conform to the environmental regulations of the country of origin.

Printed and bound in August 2023 by
CPI Group (UK) Ltd, Croydon, CR0 4YY.

MIX
Paper | Supporting
responsible forestry
FSC® C171272

CONTENTS

Introduction

What do you get if you cross a skunk with an owl?

A bird that stinks but doesn't give a hoot.

Welcome to this fart-tastic collection of the grossest jokes for funny kids.

In this book you will find over 300 revolting rib-ticklers that will have you laughing your smelly socks off – from gag-worthy gags and loo-based LOLs to animal antics and pooey puns.

If these jokes don't tickle your funny bone then nothing will. Don't forget to share your favourites with your friends and family and have them howling with laughter, too!

FART FUNNIES

What did the poo say to the fart?

"You blow me away."

What did the fart say to the poo?

"I'll help you out."

Friend 1: "How dare you fart in front of my grandma!"

Friend 2: "I'm sorry, I didn't know it was her turn."

What's invisible and smells of worms?

A bird's fart.

Why did the fart have to leave school?

It got expelled.

What do you call a teacher who never farts in public?

A private tooter.

7

How do you know if a clown has farted?

There's a funny smell.

When should you stop telling fart jokes?

When people tell you they stink.

What do you get if you eat onions with beans?

Tear gas.

Why should you never fart in a lift?

Because it's wrong on so many levels.

What do ninjas and farts have in common?

They can both be silent but deadly.

What did the can of beans say to its dad on Father's Day?

"You're the world's best farter."

What's the smelliest kind of jacket?

A windbreaker.

What did the fart joke say to the poo joke?

"I feel like people are laughing at us."

I've just released my own fragrance ...

... but nobody else in the car liked it.

I lost my job delivering leaflets on how not to fart.

It was going great until I let one rip.

I promised I'd never tell another fart joke ...

... but sometimes they just sneak out.

Knock, knock!

Who's there?

Ife.

Ife, who?

Ife-arted, sorry about that.

Knock, knock!

Who's there?

Ibroke.

Ibroke, who?

Ibroke wind, you'll smell it in a second.

Knock, knock!

Who's there?

Hoof.

Hoof, who?

Hoof-arted? It stinks in here.

Where can you buy anti-fart medicine?

At the defartment store.

Why did no one laugh when the king farted?

Because it was a noble gas.

Why did the driver fart?

To give the car a
little more gas.

**What did the winner of the
farting competition say?**

"I knew I had it in me."

**How do you turn a bath
into a bubble bath?**

Eat beans for dinner.

Why did the spy never fart in bed?

Because it would blow his cover.

What's it called when a dinosaur farts?

A blast from the past.

Why did the fart cross the road?

Because it was stuck in the chicken's pants.

SILLY SNOT

What did the finger say to the snot?

"I'd pick you first."

What did the snot say to the finger?

"Pick on someone your own size."

What did the nose say to the finger?

"Stop picking on me."

17

What did the snot say to the desk?

"I'm stuck on you."

What's another name for a snail?

A snot wearing a crash helmet.

What's the difference between a prince and a snot?

A prince is an heir to the throne. A snot is thrown to the air.

What's a snot's favourite restaurant?

Booger King.

What do you call a piece of cheese stuck up your nose?

A cheese-booger.

I thought there was something in my nose ...

... but when I looked in the mirror there was snot.

19

What's the difference between snot and broccoli?

Kids don't eat broccoli.

Why was the documentary on snot so popular?

It was engrossing.

Why should you never eat bogeys at a restaurant?

Because they're snot on the menu.

What did one bogey say to the other?

"You think you're funny, but you're snot."

What comes out of your nose at 150 mph?

A Lambo-greeny.

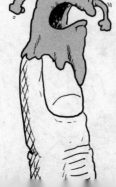

What monster can fit on the end of your finger?

The bogeyman.

ACHOOOO!

What do you call a bogey in space?

An astro-snot.

Why don't snowmen like eating carrot cake?

It reminds them of their snots.

Cleaning up snot is not funny.

It's a very serious tissue.

How much does the
average bogey weigh?

Snot much.

What do you call
a skinny snot?

Slim pickings.

I've been accused of lying about
how much snot comes out of
my nose when I sneeze.

People say I'm blowing
it out of proportion.

23

Did you pick your nose?

No, I was born with it.

How do you make a tissue dance?

Put some boogey in it.

Which sailors are always blowing their noses?

Anchor chiefs.

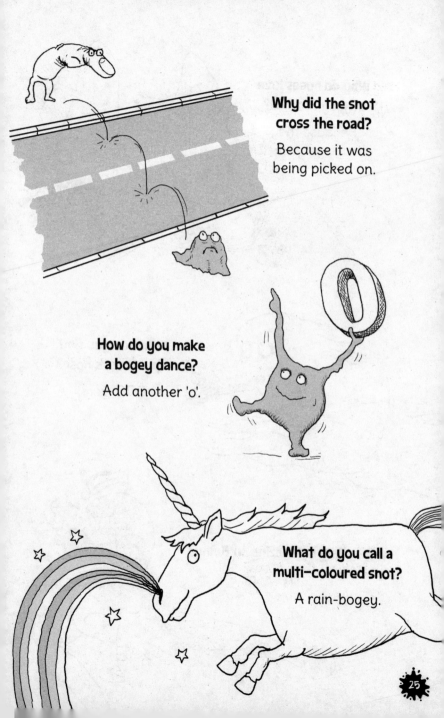

Why did the snot cross the road?

Because it was being picked on.

How do you make a bogey dance?

Add another 'o'.

What do you call a multi-coloured snot?

A rain-bogey.

Why do noses love playing football?

Because they always get picked.

What do you find up a ghost's nose?

BOO-gers.

Why is sneezing so funny?

It's snot.

26

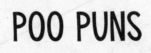

POO PUNS

Poo jokes aren't my favourite jokes ...

... but they're a solid number two.

Why did the baker have smelly hands?

Because he kneaded a poo.

I met a mountain lion once ...

... it made me puma pants!

**What's brown
and sticky?**

A stick.

**What's brown
and sounds
like a bell?**

Dung!

**What do you call
a mystery poo?**

A poo-dunnit.

**What do you call
a magical poo?**

Poodini.

**What did the poo
say to the wee?**

"Let's go out together."

30

What kind of poo smells better than it tastes?

Shampoo.

What's a toilet's favourite breakfast?

Poo-ridge.

I was picking up some dog poo in the park today and I thought to myself ...

... I really should get a dog.

What did one poo say to the other poo?

"You look flushed."

What did one dung beetle say to the other dung beetle?

"Excuse me, is this stool taken?"

I just pooped my pants ...

... which is weird, because
I don't remember
eating them.

**What's the worst thing
about poo jokes?**

They're corny.

**What did the farmer
do when he ran out
of manure?**

He had to make
doo doo.

Knock, knock!

Who's there?

I eat mop.

I eat mop, who?

You eat your poo? Gross!

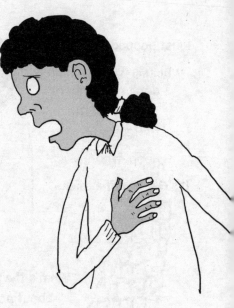

Knock, knock!

Who's there?

Smell mop.

Smell mop, who?

Yuck, no thanks!

Knock, knock!

Who's there?

Poop.

Poop, who?

It's OK, I went earlier.

Knock, knock!

Who's there?

Europe.

Europe, who?

No, you're a poo!

Did you hear about National Diarrhoea Week?

It runs until Friday.

Did you hear the song about poo?

It got to number two.

Did you know that diarrhoea is hereditary?

It runs in the jeans.

Did you hear about the giant with diarrhoea?

It's all over town.

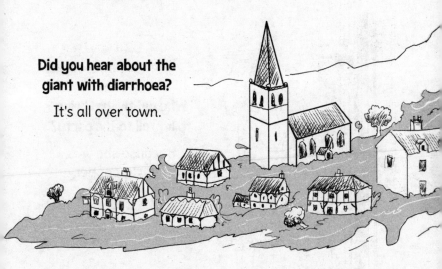

Friend 1: "Every time I go to that restaurant I get diarrhoea".

Friend 2: "Try ordering the cheeseburger next time".

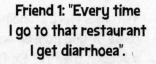

Why did the girl bring toilet roll to the party?

Because she was a party pooper.

Two flies were standing on a piece of dog poo, when all of a sudden the first fly farted.

"Do you mind?" said the second fly. "I'm trying to eat!"

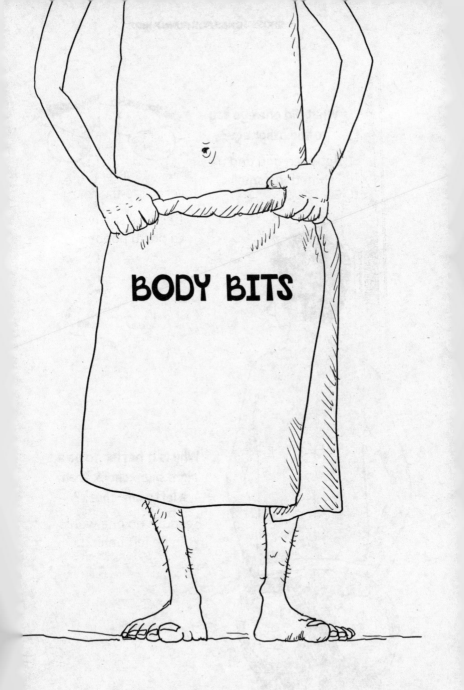

BODY BITS

What did one eye say to the other eye?

"Between you and me, something smells."

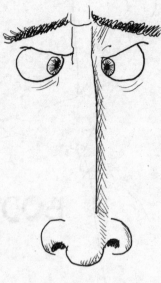

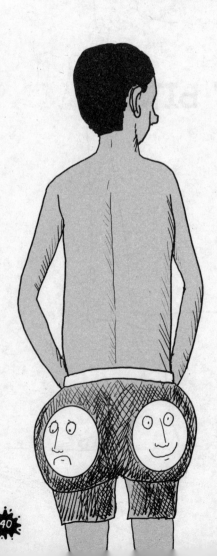

Why is it better to be a right bum-cheek than a left bum-cheek?

Because no one wants to be left behind.

Why did the man try to get a refund for his bum?

Because it had a crack in it.

Did you hear about the man who installed a window in his rear end?

It was a pane in the bum.

What's the last thing that goes through a fly's mind when it hits a car windscreen?

Its bum.

Why do basketball players have soggy carpets?

Because they're always dribbling.

What did the cop say to the belly button?

"You're under a vest."

How do you stop your nose from running?

Take away its shoes.

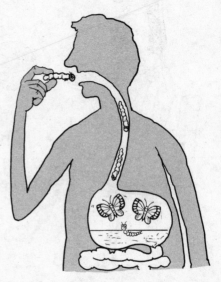

I've got butterflies in my tummy ...

... that's the last time I eat caterpillars.

Why can't a nose be 12 inches long?

Because then it would be a foot.

What do you call a nose with no body?

Nobody nose.

"Doctor, Doctor, my nose runs and my feet smell."

"I think you might have been built upside-down."

Why was the nose tired?

Because it had been running.

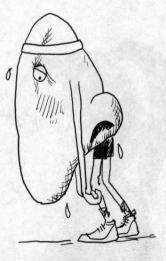

What do you find in a clean nose?

Fingerprints.

What happened to the witch whose nose was upside-down?

Every time she sneezed, her hat blew off.

What's another name for a nose?

A double-barrel snot gun.

What goes "haha thump"?

A man laughing his head off.

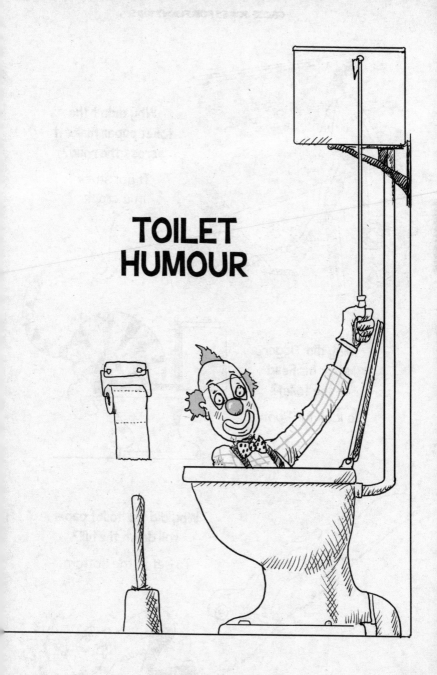

TOILET
HUMOUR

Why didn't the toilet paper make it across the road?

It got stuck in a crack.

Why did Tigger stick his head in the toilet?

To look for Pooh.

Why did the toilet paper roll down the hill?

To get to the bottom.

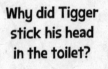

Did you hear about the film *Constipated*?

It never came out.

Why were there balloons in the bathroom?

Because there was a birthday potty.

49

What did the toilet paper say when it was feeling tired?

"I'm just wiped."

My turn!

What are the two reasons why you should never drink from a toilet?

Number one and number two.

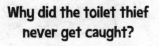

Why did the toilet thief never get caught?

Because the police had nothing to go on.

What do you find in the captain's toilet?

The captain's log.

Why did the witches need a plumber?

Hubble bubble, toilet trouble.

What's the one thing worse than a cold toilet seat?

A warm toilet seat.

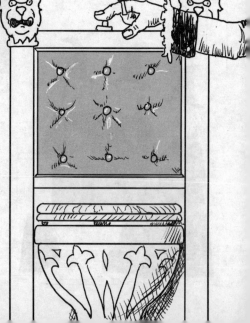

What does the king do after using the toilet?

A royal flush.

I went to the bathroom and took a poo ...

... I don't know whose poo it was, but it's mine now.

What's the difference between a toilet and a sink?

If you don't know, you're not coming round to my house.

Why should you call your toilet "the Jim" instead of "the John"?

So that you can say you go to the Jim every morning.

I was in the supermarket and a stack of toilet rolls fell on top of me.

Luckily, it was just soft tissue damage.

Where should you go if the swimming pool toilet is closed?

Deep-ends.

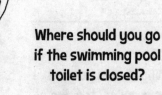

What happens if you try to flush wooden shoes down the toilet?

The toilet gets clogged.

What should you say if you find a toilet in heaven?

"Halle-LOO-yah!"

Hurry up in there, Wellington!

What train station should you go to if you need the toilet?

Waterloo.

55

What's your IP address?

The bathroom.

What does Batman say when he needs the loo?

"To the batroom!"

Where does Vin go after eating a super-hot curry?

Da loo.

**What do you call a
toilet made of ice?**

An ig-loo.

**What do you call an
igloo without a toilet?**

An ig.

Did you hear about the girl who cleaned the toilet with her younger brother?

Their mum came in and yelled, "Get his head out of there!"

Do you know the difference between toilet paper and a shower curtain?

Oh, so it's you then.

Why did no one like the toilet joke?

I guess you had to pee there.

Where does a toilet write down its secrets?

In its diarrhoea.

What do you call a soldier who spends all day on the toilet?

A loo-tenant.

What starts with a 't', ends with a 't' and is full of 'p'?

A toilet.

What starts with a 'Q' and ends with a 'P'?

A busy public toilet.

What kind of plants grow in bathrooms?

Toilet-trees.

"Mum, can I lick the bowl?"

"No, use the flush like everyone else!"

What's the difference between toilet paper and toast?

Toast gets brown on both sides.

What two things is the inventor of the toilet remembered for?

Number one and number two.

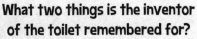

ZOMBIE ZINGERS

What do you call a zombie who never laughs?

Dead serious.

Why can't zombies be arrested?

Because you'll never take them alive.

Why did the zombie stay home from school?

Because she was feeling rotten.

**What room are
zombies banned from?**

The living room.

**Why did the zombie get
caught for speeding?**

He left his foot
on the pedal.

**What's a zombie's
favourite month?**

Dismember.

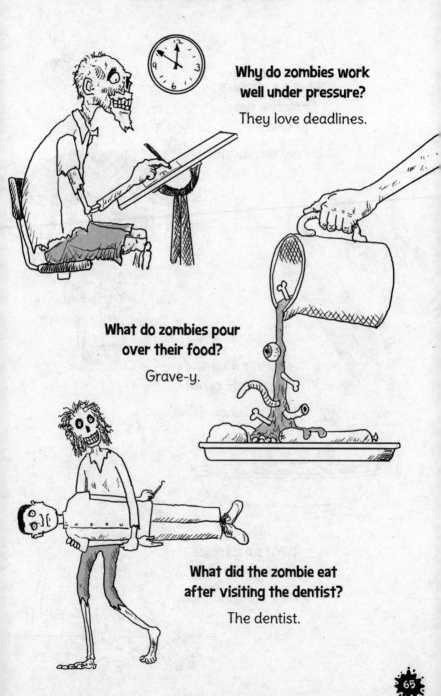

Why do zombies work well under pressure?

They love deadlines.

What do zombies pour over their food?

Grave-y.

What did the zombie eat after visiting the dentist?

The dentist.

What's a zombie's favourite type of weather?

A braaaaaainstorm.

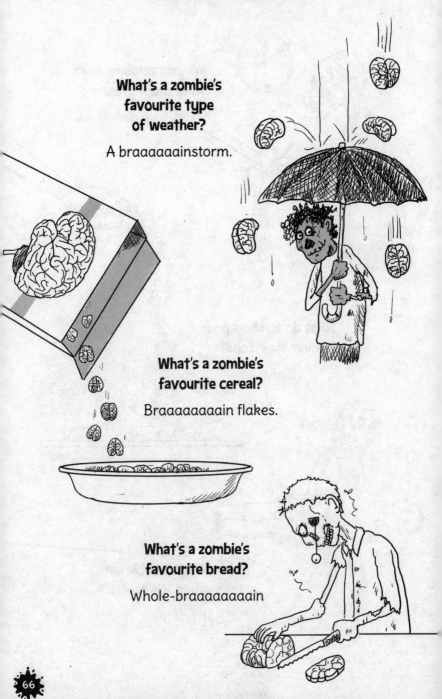

What's a zombie's favourite cereal?

Braaaaaaaain flakes.

What's a zombie's favourite bread?

Whole-braaaaaaaain

What do vegetarian zombies eat?

Graaaaaaains.

What do zombie pirates eat?

Arrrrrrms.

What do you call a zombie father?

The walking dad.

What did the polite zombie say after being introduced?

"Pleased to eat you."

Why did the zombie eat a light bulb?

Because he wanted to have a light snack.

What's the best way to speak to an angry zombie?

From as far away as possible.

Why don't zombies eat popcorn with their fingers?

They prefer to eat the fingers separately.

What did the zombie say when he got into a fight?

"Do you want a piece of me?"

Where do zombies live?

On dead-end streets.

**Where do zombies
like to swim?**

In the Dead Sea.

**What's a zombie's
favourite shampoo?**

Dead and Shoulders.

What's a zombie's favourite cheese?

Zom-brie.

What did the zombie say when she was feeling tired?

"I'm dead on my feet."

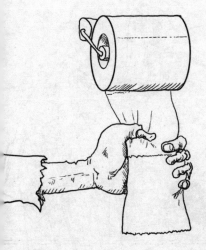

What did the zombie do after dumping his friend?

He wiped his bum.

Why did the zombie chase the archer?

To get to his bone and marrow.

Why did the zombie fail the job interview?

Because they wanted someone more lively.

Why did the zombie go to the doctor?

Because of his coffin.

What's a zombie's favourite kind of bean?

A human bean.

What's a zombie's favourite toy?

A deady bear.

What did the zombie get when he was late for dinner?

The cold shoulder.

What do zombies do at weddings?

Toast the bride and groom.

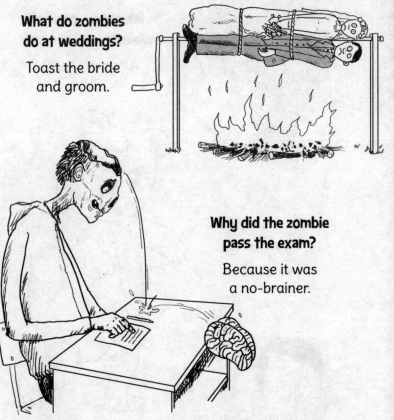

Why did the zombie pass the exam?

Because it was a no-brainer.

Two zombies are eating a clown.

One says to the other, "Does this taste funny to you?"

Why didn't the zombie go on the rollercoaster?

Because he didn't have the guts.

What's black, white and dead all over?

A zombie in a tuxedo.

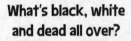

What's a zombie's favourite food?

You!

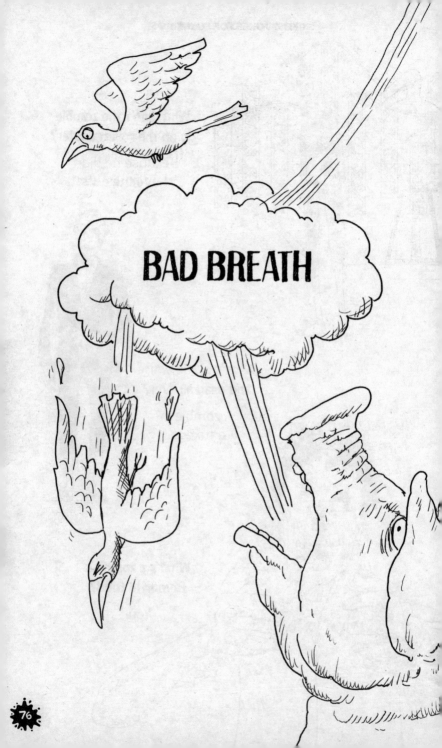

BAD BREATH

How do scientists freshen their breath?

With experi-mints.

Why did the vampire need mouthwash?

He had bat breath.

What do cannibals eat to keep their breath fresh?

Men-toes.

What do you call a frail old wizard with blisters and bad breath?

A super-calloused fragile mystic hexed by halitosis.

What do you give a nervous person with bad breath?

Encourage-mint.

What do you give a mouse with bad breath?

Mouse-wash.

What should you do if your breath smells?

Hold your nose.

What do flats eat when they have bad breath?

Apart-mints.

Why did the angel's breath smell?

She had halo-tosis.

PEE-PEE
TEE-HEES

If you like pee jokes ...

... urine luck!

**Why can't you hear
a pterodactyl going
to the bathroom?**

Because the
pee is silent.

**What happened to
the fly when it landed
on the toilet seat?**

It got peed off.

If you're American in the living room, what are you in the bathroom?

European.

Why was the sand wet?

Because the sea weed.

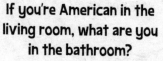

What did the pee say when it won the race?

"I'm number one!"

What do you call a country where everyone pees at the same time?

A uri-nation.

What happens if you pee on a police car?

Urine trouble.

What did the man say when he peed into the wind?

"It's all coming back to me now."

What happened to the top-secret pee joke?

Someone leaked it.

What's the difference between seafood and pea soup?

You can see food but you can't pea soup.

When it comes to peeing, on a scale of one to ten ...

... you're an eight!

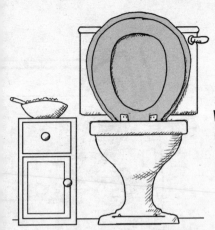

Why should you never aim your pee inside the bowl?

Because it'll ruin your cereal.

If a demon is forcing you to drink pee, where are you?

Urine hell.

What should you do if you forget to pee before a long car journey?

Forever hold your pees.

What did the French man say when he needed to pee?

"Oui!"

Why can't countries stop peeing?

Because they're in-continents.

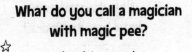

What do you call a magician with magic pee?

A whizz-ard.

"Doctor, Doctor, it hurts when I pee. What's going on?"

"Urine pain."

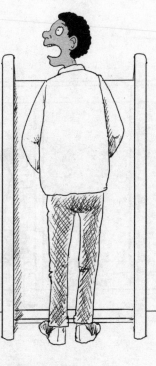

What did the boy shout when he peed all the way down the water slide?

"Weeeeeeeeeeeeeee!"

Why do gardeners have wet trousers?

Because they're always soiling their plants.

Knock, knock!

Who's there?

Peep.

Peep, who?

Pee AND poo? Make your mind up!

Why are friends like ice cubes?

If you pee on them, they'll disappear.

Why did eight pee on seven?

Because seven said,
"You're an eight."

What's the only thing worse than waking up to pee 30 minutes before your alarm goes off?

Not waking up.

Where do volcanoes go to pee?

The lava-tory.

What did you have for breakfast?

Pea soup.

What did you have for lunch?

Pea soup.

What did you have for dinner?

Pea soup.

What did you have for supper?

Pea soup.

What did you do all night?

Pee soup.

What do you call a stool you stand on to pee?

A streaming platform.

What does a pirate do when you take a pee?

He becomes irate.

How do you know if your pee is lying to you?

You can see right through it.

What did the pee club say to its newest member?

"Urine!"

How does a vegetable pee?

With its Brussels spout.

What did Shakespeare say when he wasn't sure if he needed to go to the toilet or not?

"To pee, or not to pee? That is the question."

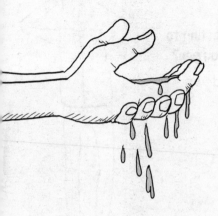

Why should you never hold your pee?

Because your hands will get wet.

Why do people pee in the shower?

Because peeing in the bath is disgusting.

What comes after a pee?

A 'Q'.

What's worse than forgetting to pull your zip up after you pee?

Forgetting to pull it down before you pee.

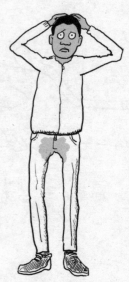

Where do bees go to pee?

The BP station.

Why did the star pee on the planet?

Because it needed to twinkle.

AWFUL
ANIMALS

Why do gorillas have such big nostrils?

Because they have such big fingers.

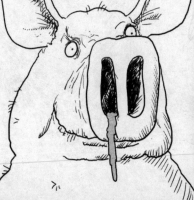

What do you do if you find a bear in your toilet?

Let it finish.

What do you get if you pick a pig's nose?

A ham-booger.

What do you call a cat who eats beans?

Puss 'n' toots.

What's invisible and smells of carrots?

Rabbit farts.

Friend 1: "Can I still sell my kayak equipment if my dog has peed on it"?

Friend 2: "You mean, can you peddle a paddle if it's in a puddle of poodle piddle?"

Why does a giraffe like having a long neck?

Because its feet smell.

What's in the middle of a gummy bear?

A jelly button.

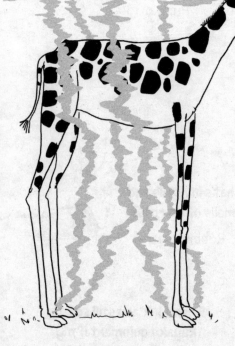

How do you tell one end of a worm from the other?

Put it in a bowl of flour and wait for it to fart.

Why did the poo cross the road?

Because it was stuck to the chicken's foot.

What's the worst thing that can happen to a bat while its asleep?

Diarrhoea.

How do elephants flush the toilet?

By peeing in it.

Farmer 1: "Horse manure is excellent for strawberries."

Farmer 2: "You might be right, but I still prefer whipped cream."

How can you tell if a cow has farted?

Check its dairy-air.

How does a cow poo?

It has a bowel moooooooovement.

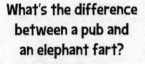

**What's the difference
between a pub and
an elephant fart?**

One is a bar room,
the other is a
BAHHHH-ROOOOOM!

**What do you call a
pile of frog poo?**

Toadstools.

Why was the duck wearing pants?

To cover its bum quack.

What do you call an ox with a big bum?

A butt-ox.

What kind of animal has two grey feet and two brown feet?

An elephant with diarrhoea.

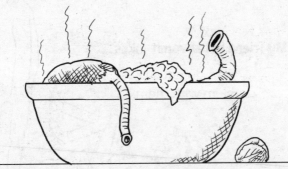

GAGS TO MAKE YOU GAG

My friend hates vomit jokes ...

... but I do nausea
problem with them.

**Why did the vomiting class
have to be cancelled?**

Something came up.

**What should you say to
someone who throws up
during a conversation?**

"I'm glad you
brought that up."

What do you call a pilot who does too many loop-the-loops?

Puke Skywalker.

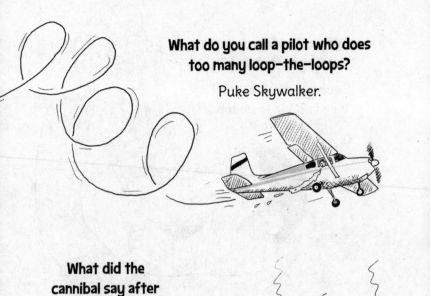

What did the cannibal say after throwing up?

"You can't keep a good man down."

Why should you never throw up Scrabble pieces?

Because they could spell trouble.

**Why will eating chairs
make you throw up?**

Because they don't sit
well in your stomach.

**Why did the woman throw
up after eating chickpeas?**

Because they made
her falafel.

"Doctor, Doctor, every time I open my eyes I throw up".

"Sounds like a case of see sickness."

What's it called when you're on your own in Spain and you throw up?

Barf-alone-a.

Why did the basketball player throw up?

Because that's where the hoop is.

What do you call a smelly fairy?

Stinkerbell.

What's the world's smelliest game?

Top Trumps.

What has four wheels and flies?

A rubbish truck.

How many rotten eggs does it take to make a stink bomb?

A phew!

What's the smelliest city in America?

Phew York.

Why do churches stink?

Because of all the pews.

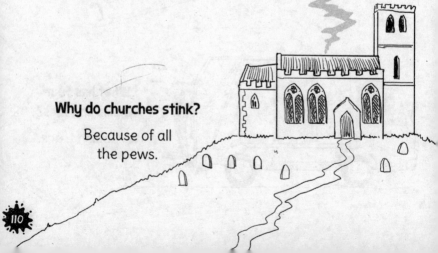

**What did one snowman
say to the other?**

"Can you smell carrots?"

**What stinks and
rhymes with "boo!"?**

You!

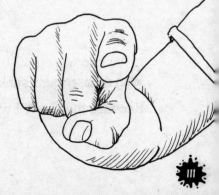

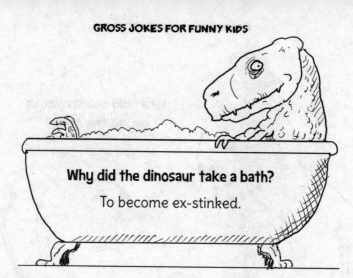

Why did the dinosaur take a bath?

To become ex-stinked.

Everyone tells me nose jokes stink ...

... but I think eye jokes are cornea.

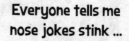

Why do laser guns stink?

Because they go "PEW"!

Why does no one like going near millionaires?

Because they're stinking rich.

Friend 1: "I've decided to go and live with a pig."

Friend 2: "Are you crazy? What about the stink"?

Friend 1: "I'm sure the pig will get used to it."

What's strong and smelly?

A piece of cheese lifting weights.

BURPS, BELCHES
AND BELLY LAUGHS

What did the stomach say to the burp?

"If you're nice and quiet I'll let you go out the back door."

Why did the skeleton burp?

Because it didn't have the guts to fart.

What happens if you burp in front of a king?

You're given a royal pardon.

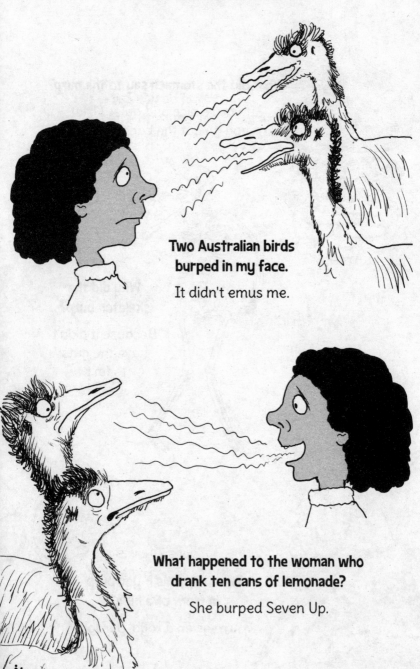

**Two Australian birds
burped in my face.**

It didn't emus me.

**What happened to the woman who
drank ten cans of lemonade?**

She burped Seven Up.

What do you call a cowboy with wind?

Wyatt Burp.

What colour is a belch?

Burple.

What happens if you burp and fart at the same time?

You take a screenshot of your body.

Why fart and waste it ...

... when you can burp
and taste it?

**Why did nobody watch the
documentary about burping?**

Because it was a repeat.

**What's got two
thumbs and burps?**

Daaaaaaaaad!

STINKY
SKUNKS

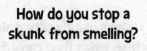

How do you stop a skunk from smelling?

Put a peg on its nose.

Did you hear the joke about the skunk?

Never mind, it stinks.

Skunks don't make dollars ...

... they make scents.

Three skunks were walking along together, when they came to a fork in the road.

The first skunk said, "My instincts tell me to go left."

The second skunk said, "My instincts tell me to go right."

The third skunk said, "My end stinks too, but it's not telling me anything."

Why did the man want a refund for his pet skunk?

Because it didn't make scents.

What do you get if you cross a skunk with a chicken?

A fowl smell.

What do you get if you cross a skunk with an owl?

A bird that stinks but doesn't give a hoot.

What do you get if you cross a skunk with a judge?

Law and odour.

What did the animal trainer say when he finally got his skunk to perform a trick?

"Eureka!"

How do skunks know when to use their spray?

Instincts.

What did the skunk say when it went to church?

"Let us spray."

Why did the skunk cross the road?

To get to the odour side.

Why can't skunks keep secrets?

Because someone always catches wind of them.

What do you call a skunk that is flying through the air?

A smellicopter.

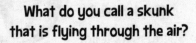

**Where did the skunk
sit in church?**

On a pew.

**Why did the kid bring
a skunk to school?**

For Show and Smell.

**Why did the skunk
call a plumber?**

Because its toilet
was out of odour.

What do you get if you cross a skunk with a Christmas bell?

Jingle Smells.

Why did the skunk buy a big box of tissues?

Because it had a stinking cold.

What do you call a dead skunk?

A stunk.